Vivaldi Classic
User Guide

Software Version 4.06.xx

© 2014 - **Vivaldi Systems**

www.vivaldi2000.com

Corporation Phone Number: +1 (760) 524-2473
Tech Support: +1 (760) 282-4421

Sales Support: sales@vivaldisystems.com
Technical Support: support@vivaldisystems.com

Use you smartphone to access us!!

Modified 5/25/2014

Contents

Introduction

Hello and congratulations on purchasing your Vivaldi Systems Dry Cleaning Software package, designed to deliver a strong and easy-to-use Windows Software packaged for today's technology. During this introduction, I will show you what is included with this software and then immediately dive into a walkthrough towards what you will be experiencing day-to-day when you work with Vivaldi Classic.

At a Glance

With this software, you're experiencing a visual system ready for today's demands in terms of dry cleaning software. The entire user experience is designed simplistically, allowing you to access the buttons that you need when you need them.

Designed on a C++ Windows backbone, the software is capable of running on any Windows platform ranging from Windows 95 to the latest Windows 8.1 or any operating system in between.

System Requirements

If you are running Vivaldi Classic on at least a Windows 7 PC, we recommend you have at least these hardware requirements on your PC:

Windows 32bit operating system
Pentium Dual Core CPU or above
Minimum 2GB of RAM
500 MB of Hard Drive space or above. (5 GB is enough)

We strongly recommend you to purchase a 32bit system. That way you can operate the Report Writer, enabling you to customize and design your reports, tags, and tickets.

To get more installation programs included with the software package, visit www.vivaldi2000.com.

Remote Login

So receive advanced customer support, which may require remote access to you computer via Internet, we ask you to visit www.teamviewer.com and download the software.

To get more information, please go to page 65 to get a step-by-step guide to installing the software and know what we require before remoting into your system.

Chapter- 1

Basic Walkthrough

At a Glance

In order for you to get a good grasp of the software, we're gonna switch it up a bit. First we're gonna go through the basic system on a regular day. Once we're done with this chapter, we'll explain detail-to-detail what each of the different button and modules do. So let's begin by following the steps to follow what a typical counter person would need to do on a regular basis.

The Vivaldi About

When you first open Vivaldi Classic for the first time, whether it'd be because you just purchased the software or just upgrading from our website, the Vivaldi About windows should appear, along with the version number. You can obviously turn off the window when you log in by clicking the appropriate checkbox labeled as "Do Not Show This Message Again." This window can be displayed by going into the software, going into the **Vivaldi About** under the **Help** menu.

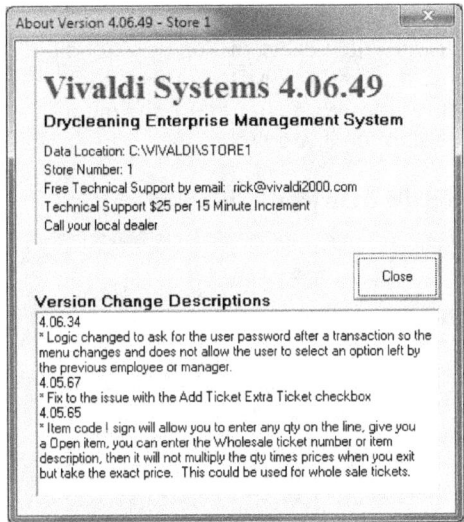

Vivaldi Wizard

This window is designed to get your basic configuration set for your system. You may answer the **Yes** or **No** questions and pressing **Next** to continue. To stop the wizard from coming up every time you enter Vivaldi Classic, check the "Do Not

Show this Setup Wizard Again." This option is meant for first-time users. You can rerun the wizard from the **Utilities** menu and go down to **Setup Wizard** option.

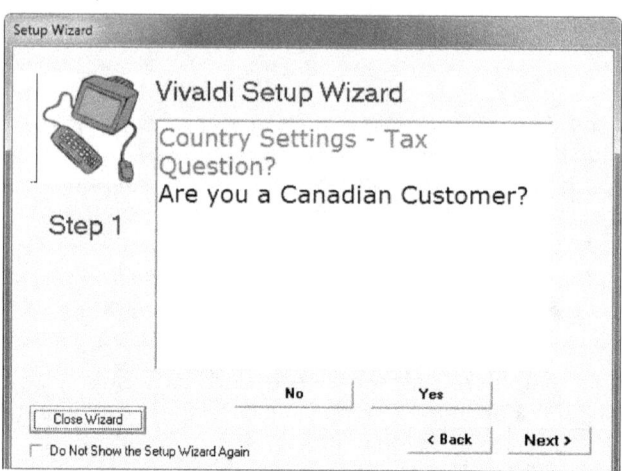

Main Menu

The picture below is something you will see on a daily basis. It's the central hub of your dry cleaning daily duties. Here you will write tickets, pickup tickets, edit tickets, accounts, etc.... Not only can you use the fuction keys to better access the buttons, but you can use you touchscreen monitor to better use the menu options. Using the mouse is also a defaulted option if you prefer.

To begin, let's assume that we have opened the store for the first time in the

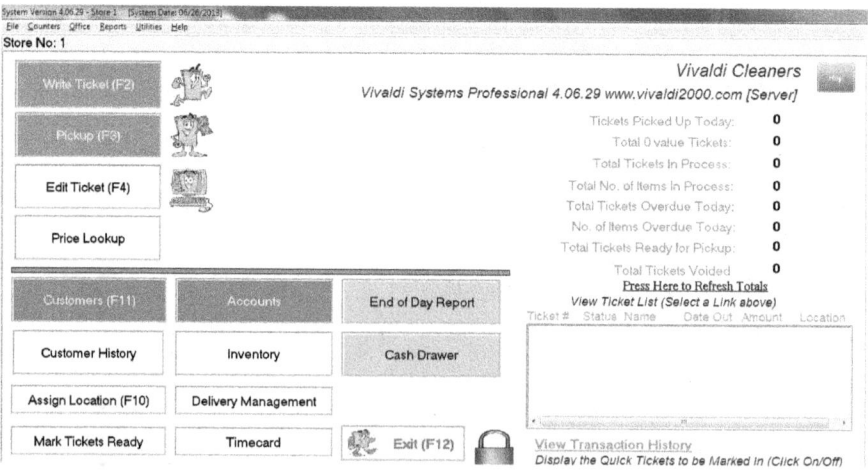

morning and we are ready to begin writing tickets. Lets' set it up in a step-by-step style.

Step 1: The Business

To begin, lets make sure the cashbox is cleared out and the starting cash is entered by following these steps.

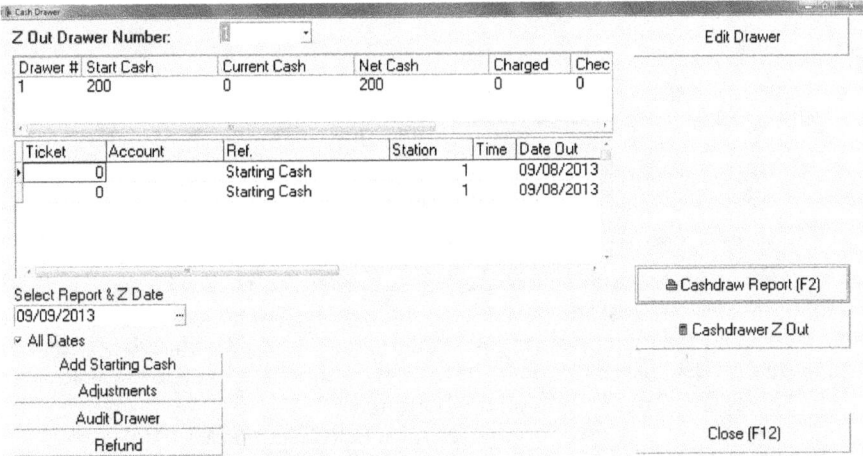

1. Press the **Cashdrawer** button on the **Main Menu** which is located in the center of the screen.
2. Press the **Cashdrawer Z Out** button
3. Press **Yes** to the Z OUT question.
4. Now click **OK** on your completion window.

*This is something people tend to do on the end of the day, but for demo's sake, we are doing it at the beginning of the day. The starting cash, of course, needs to be added before we start making transactions. So let's do that

5. Click the **Add Starting Cash** button and then add your starting amount on the **Amount** field and clicking the **Update and Save Amount to Cash Drawer** button on the right. (Let's add 100 dollars on it)
6. Press the **Close** button or press F12 on your keyboard once you're done.

Step 2: Write a Ticket/ Customer Search Window

So let's pretend that a client has walked in the door with dirty dry cleaning items ready to be cleaned. That would require us to write a ticket to complete their order.

1. Click on **Write Ticket** from the top left of the main menu screen. This will prompt you to the **Customer Search Window.**

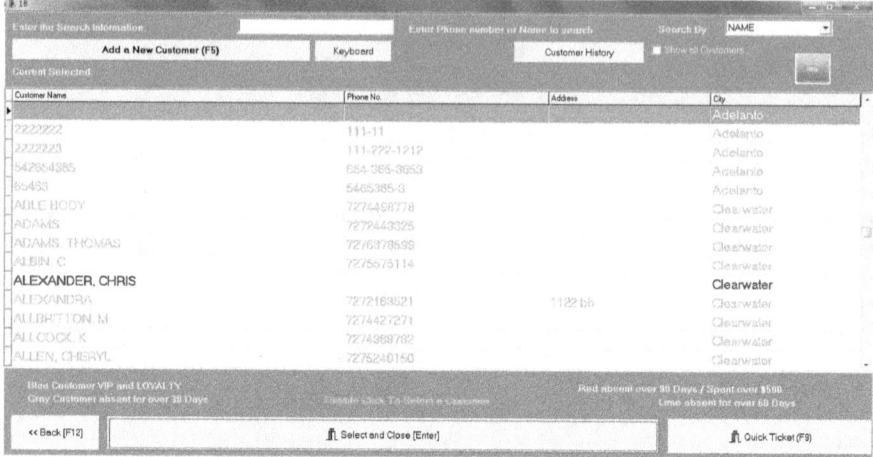

2. Enter the phone number or enter the customer's name. Vivaldi will automatically find the customer closest to what you are typing as you type.

3. When you see the customer you want to select, press the Enter key or double click on the customer's name (If you have a touchscreen, you may click the **Select and Close** button on the bottom).

4. There's also an option of printing a Quick Ticket (A ticket with only the customer's name, number of pieces and date of pickup), but we'll go into detail in a later chapter.

5. You may always go back to the main menu, by clicking the **Back** button on the left.

Step 3: Write a Ticket Window

This is the screen where you would add your items to the ticket where it would then update on the right. First things first, let's add items.

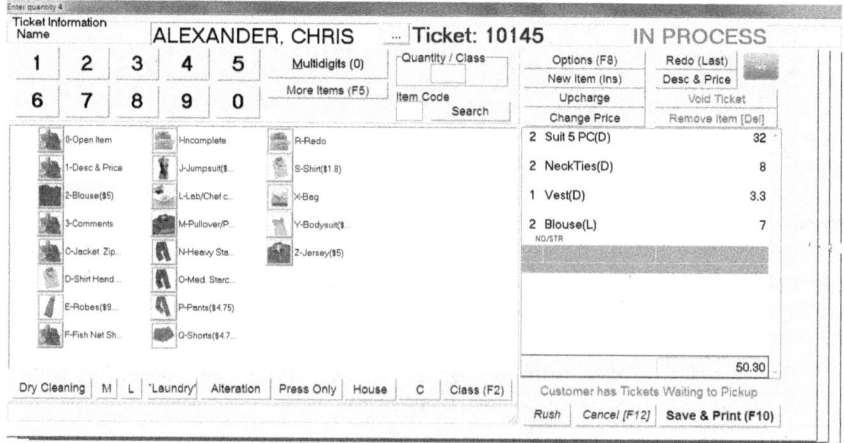

1. With Vivaldi, you would press the quantity first and then select the item from the list provided. Press the number buttons provided for you on the top left.
2. Next you would select the item from the list or use the item code (Ex: Open item : "0".) (If you only have one item, then simply click on the item. Vivaldi will default the quantity to 1.

Step 4: Optional Upcharge Window

Vivaldi has many options for writing tickets. You can choose to have Vivaldi enter the optional upcharge window immediately after you select an item (we will go into detail about this in another chapter when we go into its specific properties). You can also go into it by double clicking on the items on the ticket you wish to add upcharges. Let's do that now.

1. Double click on an item on the ticket and it will go to this window.

2. Press the color you wish and select the Upcharges you wish to add to the item. (You may select as many upcharges as you wish as well as describe an item not in the list)
3. The Color buttons at the bottom of the screen allow you to define colors and styles in addition to quick color buttons on the bottom of the window.
4. Once you're done, click **Close**, which will lead you back to the previous window.

(We will go into detail later in another chapter about adding more upcharges to your list.)

Step 5: Calendar and Print Window

Once you're done choosing the items for your ticket, you can click on **Save and Print** on the lower right of the window. This would lead you to the **Calendar** window, where you would select a date for pickup. This is how the screen looks like.

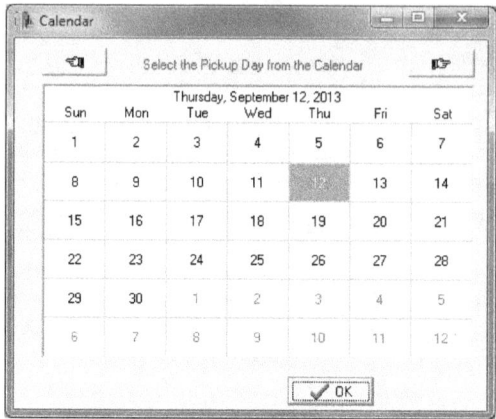

Once you've selected a date, the **Print** window should appear, loading you with an overwhelming amound of buttons and fields. Not to worry. This would get easier

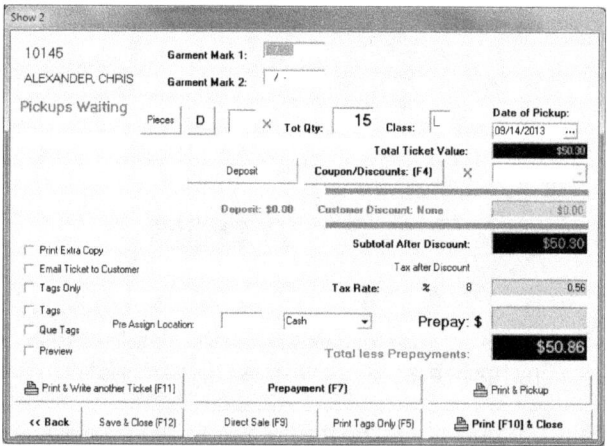

once you start using this screen over and over again. So for this demonstration, let's click **Save & Close** if you don't wish to use your ticket printer. In any other case, click **Print & Close.**

Step 5: Picking up Tickets

During the course of your day, you may be doing the things that you do best: cleaning items and marking the tickets ready (again, I will explain that in a later chapter). Next, you would be picking up tickets as people come in.

1. Click on the **Pickup** button on the main menu.
2. The **Customer Search Window** similar to the write ticket version should pop up so you can select your customer.
3. The following window should display called the **Pickup** Window. This shows all the Tickets and its status on the right, as well as the date that the ticket came in.

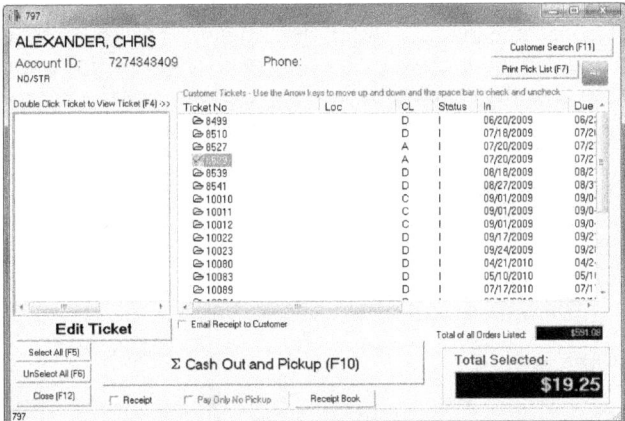

4. Click on the ticket number, which is the first column on from the left. (A red check mark should appear on the left of the Ticket No.)
5. Once you're done, click the big **Cash Out and Pick up** button on the bottom.

Step 6: Type of Payment/ Cash Tendered Window

The following screen should pop out called the **Type of Payment** window. For now, we will do the basics and click cash, which should prompt us to the **Cash Out Window.**

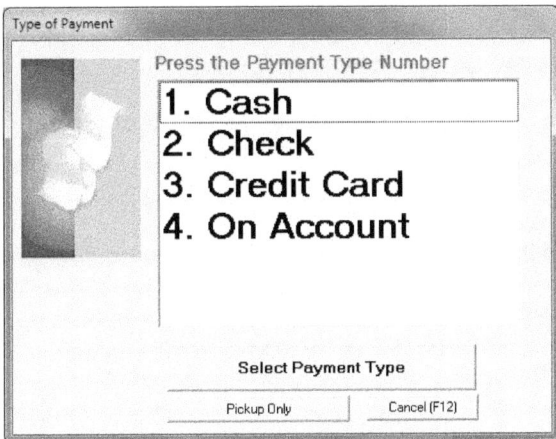

You would then select the cash tendered using the buttons provided and then click **Cash Out/ Pickup.**

Step 7: End Of Day/ Cash Reconciliation Report

In tems of your daily duties of writing and picking up tickets, you're done for the day. Now we need to move onto the cashdrawer window just like when we started this chapter. Let's go ahead and Z Out of the Drawer. When you enter the Cashdrawer Window and Z Out the drawer, click the **Cashdrawer Report** button. Go ahead and enter the quantity of coins, dollars, and the total dollar amount in checks and Vivaldi Classic will calculate the **Grand Total** for you.

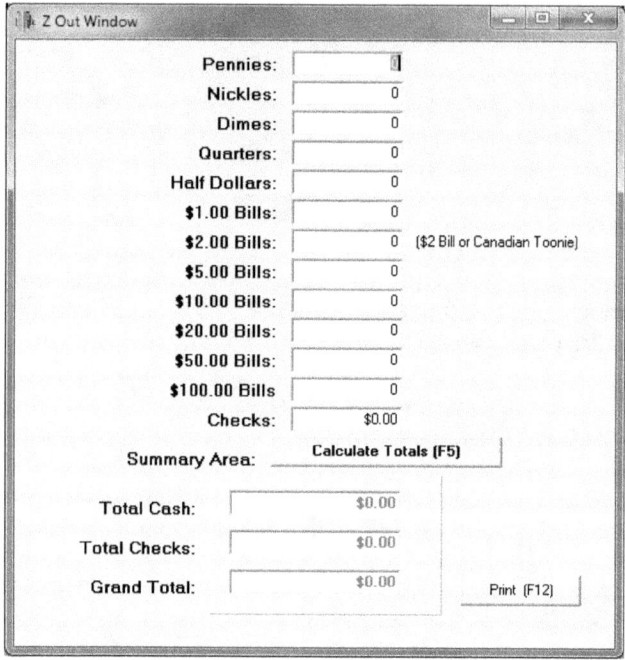

Once you're done, click the **Print** button, choose the printer and print your report for the day.

That's it! Now it's your turn.

Chapter- 2

Users and IDs

At a Glance

In this section, we will be going through the beginning of opening the software and jumping into the security section in terms of users and what level of access they may have in the system. OK, let's begin!

Optimize and Cleanup

After entering Vivaldi Classic, the program will ask if you would like to **Optimize and Cleanup** the data. You can bypass the cleanup by pressing the **Enter** button as a default. As a reminder, you should optimize and cleanup your system once a week to once a month. This message will only appear on the server system, which should appear on the top right of the main menu.

*You cannot Cleanup from a client station.
*YOU MUST EXIT ALL STATIONS FROM A NETWORK BEFORE RUNNING THE **OPTIMIZE AND CLEANUP.**

When you click **Optimize and Cleanup,** Vivaldi Classic will force you to select which store you want to cleanup, which can be done by double clicking from the list provided. Vivaldi can manage thousands of stores. After the cleanup, you will enter the store number you've just selected.

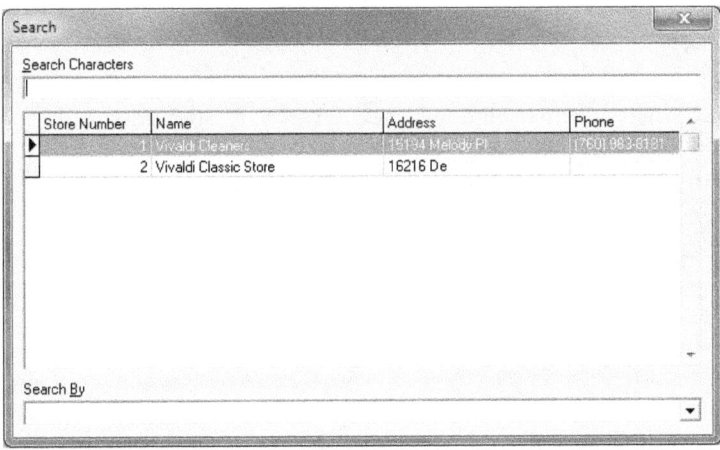

The **Optimize and Cleanup** system will remove all the indexes that speed up the searches and will rebuild them as well as pack and remove all deleted records.

Security - IDs and Passwords

This section will give you information about the built-in login identification numbers and passwords. This is used when you want to assign different IDs for each counterperson who runs your system. This could be beneficial in discovering who wrote tickets at which times of the day, which will be discussed later.

But first, we would need to activate this setting in the **System Properties**. To get to it, we would need to get to the main menu and **right click** on the whitespace or just go to **Help** and down to **System Properties**.

Store Defaults | Advanced | Other | Pickup/Store | Email | Colors |

☑ Use a DOS Tone when Ticket No. Not found

☐ Use Logins every Transaction or   ☐ Login at Opening Only

☐ Use Menu Access Control   ☐ No Upcharge for Wholesale

Under the **Store Defaults** tab, there will be three checkmark options built for the Login Setting:

> 1. **Use Logins every Transaction or**: will force user to log in after every transaction.
> 2. **Login at Opening Only**: will force you to log in only when opening the main menu.
> 3. **Use Menu Control Access**: this will limit certain users right, which will be explained shortly.

Log In Window

So what do you do when the login window appears? Well very simple actually. Just type in your password. The reason why the password is only needed is because users must select a unique user ID and therefore only the password is required. I'll explain in a bit.

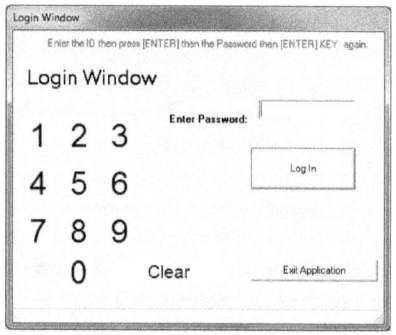

*The default user ID is 1 and the default password is 2164.

User Management

Now it's the time to create your user IDs for each of your counterpersons. Simply go to the **Utilities** menu and down to **User Management**. To create a new user, click the **New** button down on the lower left of the window. This will create a new row where you can click on the appropriate column starting with the ID typing a unique number.

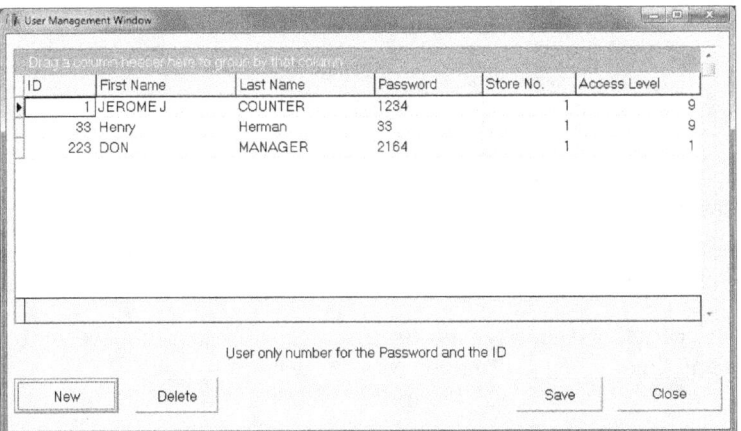

*Please use a number that is not already being used in the same column.

Then you can continue by providing the First Name, Last Name, Password, Store No. that this user ID and Password is good for, and an Access Level. Access levels must range from 1 to 9 (9 being the highest level of access. Ex: Managers would be access level 9; regular counterperson would be access level 1. Access levels would be defined in the next section called **Access Control**.

*Passwords can include numbers or characters. Please make it unique as well.

Access Control

Once you're done setting up users with their respective levels, you can now define those levels here in **Access Control**. To get there, you need to go to the **Utilities** menu and down to **Access Control.**

Select the Level 1 though 9 from the dropdown button above and then you can begin selecting the access options you wish to give that certain user using the checkmarks provided under each of the three tabs above.

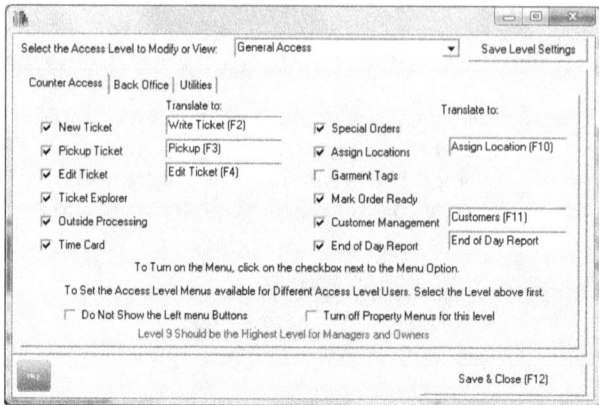

*Make sure you turn on **Use Menu Access Control** from the **System Properties** explained in the security section for this to become affective.
*Be sure to set the access level 9 for the manager to get to everything before you turn on the **Use Menu Access Control.**

Once you're done, click the **Save Level Setting** on the top right for each level and then click **Save and Close** when you're done with this window.

Chapter- 3
Write a Ticket: In Detail

At a Glance

In this chapter we will, again, go through a run at writing a ticket, but I will be jumping around different sections of the programs as to get a grasp of the different settings in the tickets menu and what the science is behind the magic.

Customer Search Window

As of this moment, I'm assuming you are familiar to getting access to the main menu and selecting the **Write Ticket** button, which should be selected so that you can see the **Customer Search Window.**

*The Customer Search Window can be accessed from the Pickup and Customer buttons on the main menu, but will work differently based on the intended purpose.

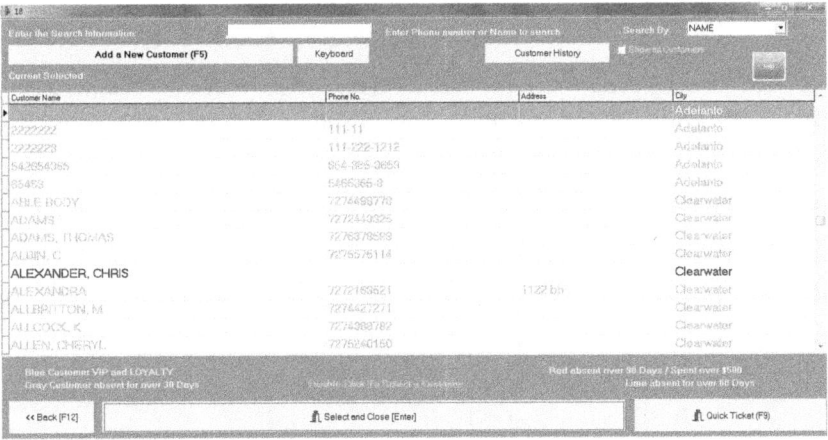

Once you begin using the system, you will start noticing different people being highlighted with different colors. These are what the colors mean:

- **Blue**: Customer is VIP and part of the Loyalty System
- **Gray**: Customer has been absent for over 30 Days, meaning he hasn't been inside the store to do a transaction for over 30 Days.
- **Red**: Customer has been absent over 90 Days and has spent over $500. This should mark a red flag for you and suggest getting in close contact with this customer.

- **Lime:** Customer has been absent for over 60 Days.

Search Type

Under the **Customer Search Window**, a customer can be found by entering either name or account number into the search box , which is defaulted to be used upon initial open. The system automatically recognizes if number or letters are entered and searches for accounts respectively.

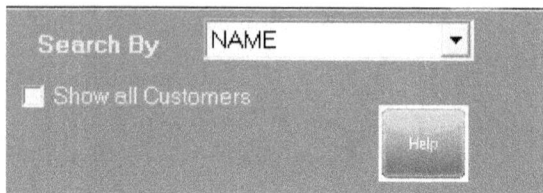

If you wish to change the search type, you can do so by clicking the dropdown button on the top right of the window labeled as **Search By**.

Adding a New Customer

So what happens when you've cleared out the data and have started from scratch and need to add new customers? Simple. Just click on **Add a New Customer** from any of the **Customer Search Window**s. The screen should look something like this.

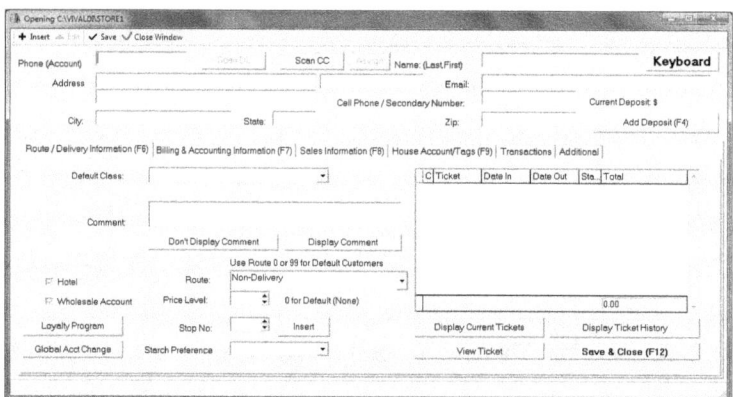

The window will appear with all text fields blank for you to enter information in them. The required information to enter a basic customer are the Account Number, which is basically a phone number, and the customer's name following the format provided (Last Name, First Name).

*If you use phone numbers for account numbers, the system will automatically populate the phone number field with the account number as you exit the account number field.

Customer Address Default

What is Customer Address Default you ask? It's the default values for the basic customer information, such as City, State, Zip Code, and the General Ledger Account. This could all be accessed in the **System Properties** window found under the **Help** menu when you're on the main menu. Let's go there now and meet you in the window that looks like this.

| Store Defaults | Advanced | Other | Pickup/Store | Email | Colors |

Customer Default Information for Adding New customers

City: Adelanto   State: CA   Zip: 92301

Default Route Number: 0   Default Area Code

Default Class Code: D

☐ Rental Mode for Tags

☐ F4 All Taxable

☑ Default to Taxable on New Customers

Under the **Advanced** tab you will see that under the "**Customer Default Information for Adding New Customer**" section you can add information that will appear as the default when adding new customer to your system.

Once you're done adding or changing the fields, click **Save** button and then the **Close** button on the bottom right of the screen.

*Remember to select save before exiting.
*Remember that these changes will need to be made on each of the stations you have and again if you have different stores.

Setting Up Tax for Customers

To begin using what we call the "Tax Module," you will need to modify several areas of Vivaldi Classic. Let's set it up in steps, shall we?

Step 1: Tax Option for New Customers

To set each new customer defaulted to taxable, let's go to the tax option line in **System Properties** under the **Help** menu. The one and only checkbox under the first section will allow you to add new customers to be taxed according to the setting at the times of their addition. Existing customer settings will not be changed. Make sure you **Save and Close** using the provided buttons below.

Step 2: Enterprise Store Management

Click **Enterprise Store Management** under the **Office** menu. Here you can include the **Tax Rate** using the text field provided. When you're done, click **Save and Close** on the bottom of the window.

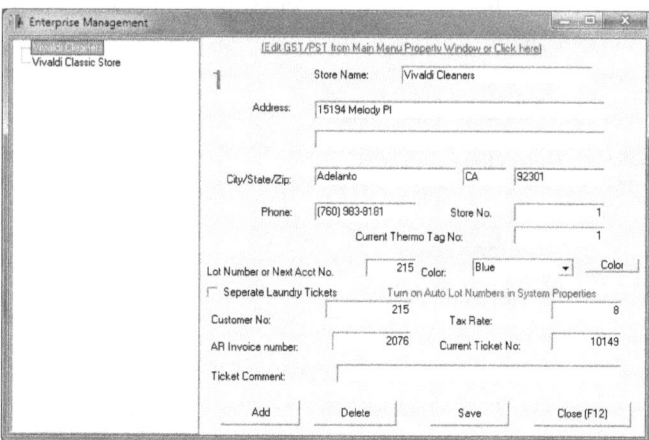

* This may be a good time to update your store information such as store name, store address, phone number and store number. Just make sure you click save when you're ready to update.

Step 3: Class Manager

As a final step, you can select which classes will have the tax rate turned on.. To get there, go to the **Utilities** menu and click **Class Manager** option. Using the checkboxes provided on the right column, you can indicate which classes are taxable

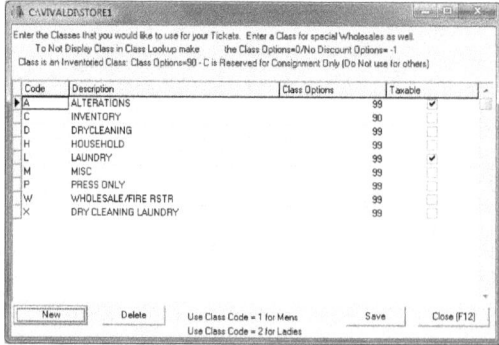

and which are not.

Add Items to the Ticket

Alright, let's get back on track in terms of writing that ticket, now that we've selected a customer from the **Customer Search Window**.

*If you've entered a Hotel Account, you must enter a Room Number and Name into the Room/Name Field. You can start entering items onto the ticket afterwards. We'll get to explain this on another chapter. Not to worry.

If you have entered a non-hotel account, the name of the customer will default into the Name field. Simply press Enter to start entering items.

Entering the Quantity of Items

If you remember in the first chapter, Vivaldi Classic requires the user to enter the quantity of items prior to selecting the type of item, but if it's only one item, you can just select the item and Vivaldi Classic will default the item to one, which will be updated onto the ticket on the right. Use the digit buttons provided above.

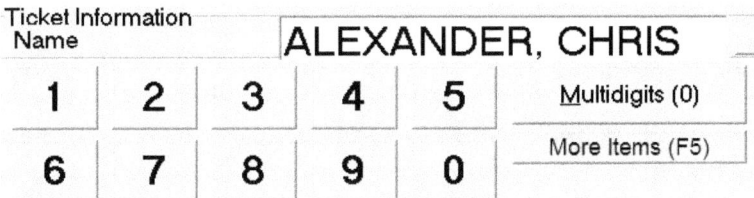

Multidigits

Let's say that you have more than 9 of the same item. It would be best to use the multidigits button or press "0" on the keyboard and the **Quantity Window** will appear.

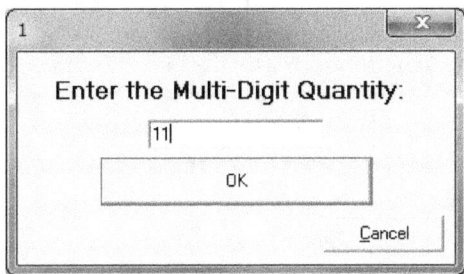

Enter the multidigit number and then press **Enter** or click **OK**. You will notice that the new number appears in the quantity field replacing the 0.

Ticket Properties

Now let's take a sneak peak at the **Ticket Properties** and see at a minimal perspective how to get to the window. Click **Ticket Properties** under the **Help** menu or you can right click on the main menu whitespace and go down to **Ticket Properties** option.

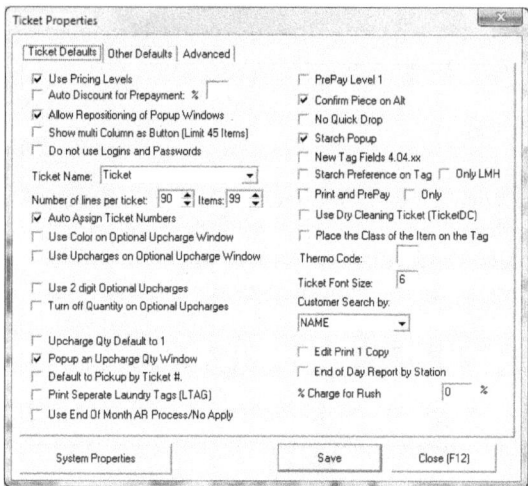

Class Options

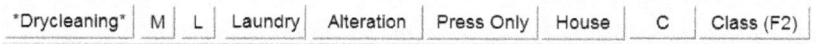

As a default in the system, the write ticket window is defaulted to class set as **Drycleaning**, noticed by the asterisks below. The bottom buttons can be used to change through the classes such as alteration, laundry, press only, and more. If you don't see the class you need to access your items, click on the **Class** button or F2 on the keyboard and you should be prompted to the **Class Selection Window**. Here you can see your available list of options. Click on the class above to Select. The item list will be refreshed.

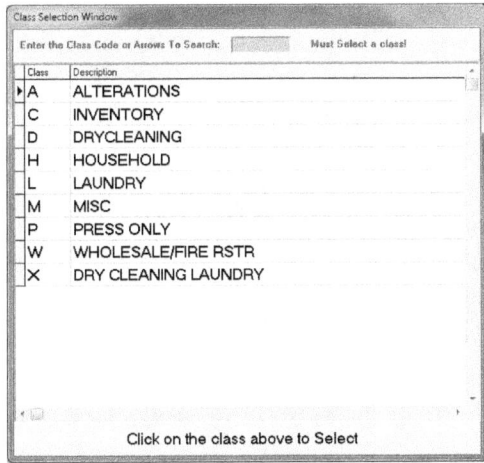

Click on the class above to Select

*I will mention about adding or modifying your classes on a later chapter. You can go there by selecting **Class Management** under the **Utilities** menu.

Selecting an Item

After the quantity is selected, the item box will appear. Press the code in either number, letter, or symbol for the item you wish to select or click on the item you wish to select. If you have a touchscreen, touch the item picture.

*I will mention about adding, modifying, and customizing items under a different chapter or you can just skip by going to **Item Management** under the **Utilities** menu.

Forced Upcharges

If you have created forced upcharges under the **Item Management** window. The upcharge list will pop up after you have selected the upcharged item. This is a forced upcharge, meaning that the user will be FORCED to select one of the options from the list.

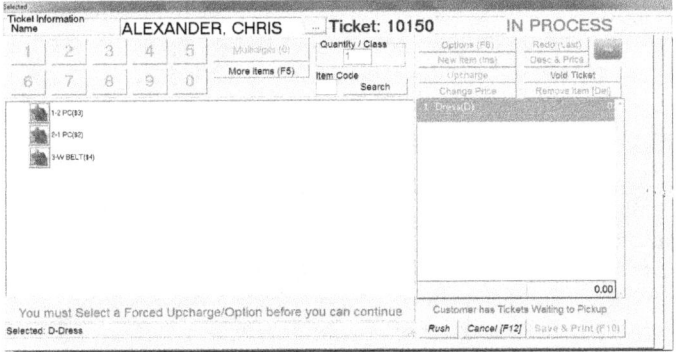

*This is not an optional upcharge. For those use the optional upcharge option.

Adding Colors to an Item

I must admit, the optional upcharge window can get a bit tricky to work around, specially if you have multiple items you want to organize using different colors. This is why I'm here: to break things down for you.

To add a color to an item, double click on the item on the ticket list on the right to access the **Optional Upcharge** window.

To select the color(s) for the item, click the small check box next to the color or press the code (1,2,3,4) when the highlist is on the Color box. The quick colors buttons on the bottom of the window will not assign an additional cost or allow you to select a quantity. These colorswill appear even if you tun off the Color Options on Optional Upcharges window.

*I will get into detail about customizing the Optional Upcharges on a later chapter. This could be accessed by going to **Optional Upcharge Management** under the **Utilities** menu.

Resizing the Windows/ Multiple Windows

Stepping back a little and relaxing from this trecherous read, I'll just sat that Vivaldi Classic is designed to be moved around in terms of window movement. To do this, you need to go to the **Ticket Properties** and the under the **Ticket Default** tab you will find the chekbox labeled "Allow Repositioning of Popup Windows" and turn on the setting.

Being a true Windows system, Vivaldi Classic will allow you to open multiple windows at once. That's why it's called Windows! Move them around and easily see what you're doing.

Printing the Ticket

Once you're done selecting the items onto the ticket for the current transaction, you can go ahead and click **Save and Print** on the bottom right of the window. You will be prompted to select a pickup date from the **Calendar** window. Once done, you will be sent to the print ticket window where you're loaded with a bunch of options in terms of what you want to do with this tickets. Options such as:
- Enter Garment Tag
- Change the number of pieces
- Enter a Coupon or Discount (Coupon Management explained later)
- Deposit Option

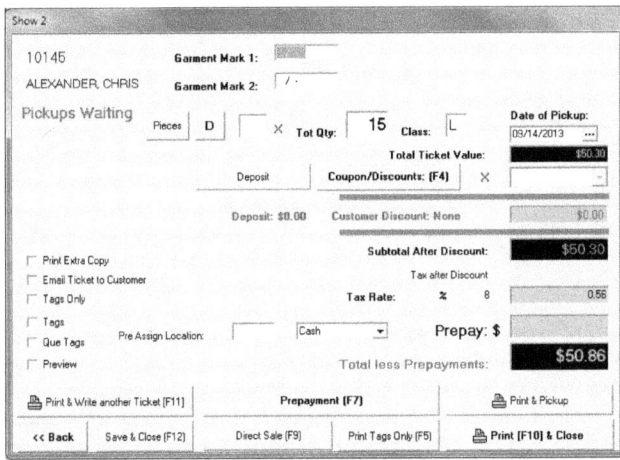

- Prepayment Option

Above all, you can preview what you're about to print using the preview window and many ways of printing tickets and tags.

Accounts Receivable Special Discounts

If the customer has a positive credit in the **Accounts Receivable** and the Price Level 1 for AR options is on, then the customer will receive the prices you've entered for the Price Level 1. You must turn on **Price Level** option under the Ticket Properties window.

*Accounts Receivable is an entirely different module and quite interesting for your customers and will be explained in detail in a later chapter. I think you'll love it once you see its potential.

Pickup Message

If the **Pickup Message** is turned on in the **System Properties** window and the customer has tickets that have been marked ready or have been assigned a location indicating they are on the rack, then the box will appear after the ticket is entered informing you that there are tickets ready for pickup. By pressing **Yes,** you will be taken automatically to the **Pickup Window** for that customer.

Chapter- 4

Edit Ticket and Picking Up Ticket: In Detail

At a Glance

In this chapter, we'll take a glance at editing tickets and picking up tickets-- a respected module in Vivaldi Classic.

Editing Tickets

After you've written a ticket and you (or the customer) wishes to modify or reprint the ticket, you need to enter the Edit Ticket window by clicking **Edit ticket** or by pressing **F4** from the **Main Menu.** You will prompted with this screen upon opening it. It is called the **Ticket Search Window.**

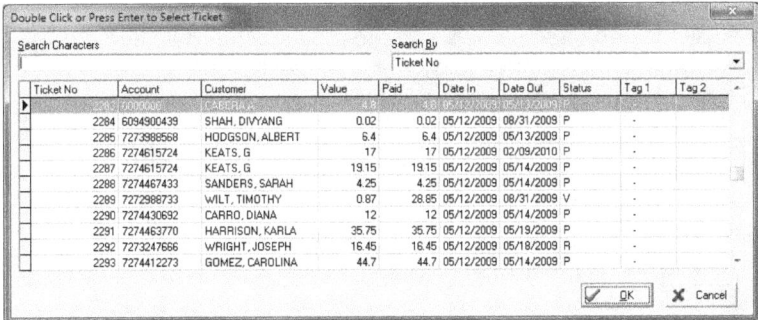

The default search is on the right. It is currently filtered as the ticket number. You can enter the ticket number using the search field provided on the left or use a different type of search using the dropdown arrow on the top right.

The other options you can search by are: Date in, Date out, Garment number, or Account.

To edit a ticket, you'll notice there is a status marking on each ticket provided by this legend:

> **P:** This is a ticket with items that have been picked up.
> **R:** This are for tickets that were marked ready
> **I:** These tickets are still in-process
> **D:** Tickets that have been deleted
> **V:** These tickets have been deleted.

29

Once you've found the ticket that you want, simply **double click** the ticket. This is the window that should appear:

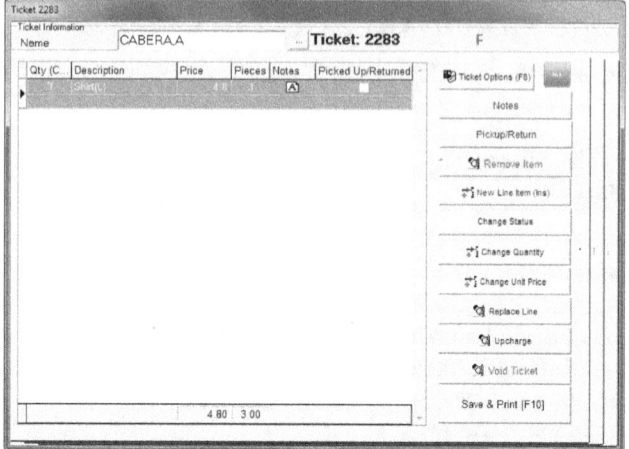

This is what we call the edit screen, where you can highlight a certain item from the item list, add notes, and remove single items from the ticket. You can change the status, quantity, the unit price, replace a line, or change the upcharge.

To reprint this ticket again, press the **Save and Print** button at the bottom right of the screen.

Picking up Tickets

When a customer has gotten a ticket processed and then you have either marked the ticket ready or assigned the location, it's time to pick up their ticket once they step through the door.

Click on **Pickup Ticket** or **F3** on the **Main Menu** and select the customer from the customer search window. If the customer is correct, you will see the number of tickets that were written. The screen does display the tickets that are currently in process and those that are not yet racket nor ready. It also displays tickets that are ready.

The ticket number will display to the left, including the class, location, status, the date the item came in, and the dat ewhen the item is ready to be picked up (indicated when you selected the date from the calendar after writing the ticket)

*If you assigned a location to the ticket, ten the location will appear on the right of the ticket number.

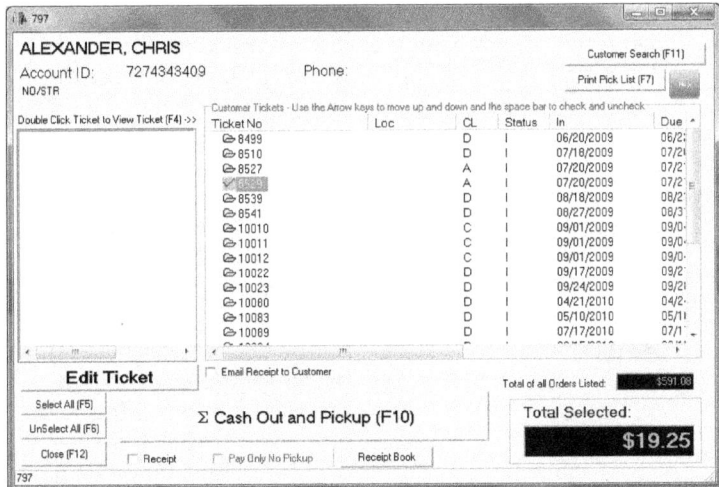

You will see various amounts of tickets written for the customer. If you double click on the ticket, the iems will appear on the left pane. As soon as you do that, you are able to edit the ticket using the button below the description. When you edit button, the ticket should come up on edit mode, which you should be familiar with after reading the previous section.

When you're done making changes, click the **Save and Print** button down on the lower part of the screen.

You also don't have to necessarily reprint the ticket, but you have the capability to do so. You can click **Save and Close.**

Once you've made any final adjustments, you can single slick the ticket, where a red checkmark will appear next to it. The total dollar amount is added onto the box down at the lower right. The total of the tickets listed will appear above in a smaller black box with the green text which says "total of all orders listed."

Total of all Orders Listed: $300.71

Total Selected:

$17.71

Finally, press the **Cashout and Pickup** button. Next you will select the form of payment. If the customer is setup as cash only because maybe they've bounced checks with you, you'll only have cash as an option. If the customer only uses checks as a form of payment, that option will be available. If this customer is an account customer, then that option will be available for them. If you have X-Charge hooked up for free credit card processing through Vivaldi and you ask for the credit card, just swipe their card and it will be processed.

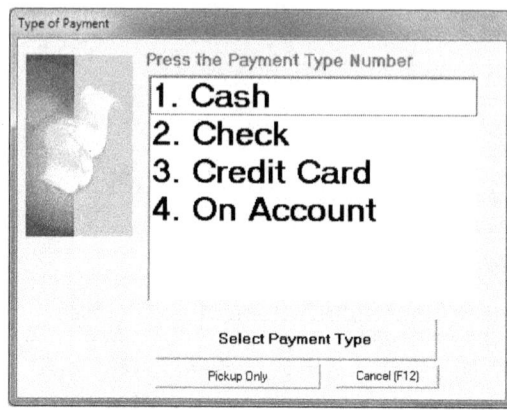

Type of Payment

Press the Payment Type Number

1. Cash
2. Check
3. Credit Card
4. On Account

Select Payment Type

Pickup Only   Cancel (F12)

Another option that Vivaldi Classic offers is to only pickup the items and pay later. The button for that option is at the bottom of the window. It will keep it on the list for the next time they come in, that they owe. I will also indicate that location is set as customer. If you've selected cash, you'll be asked for the tendered amount. You may use a tend dollar bill, twenty, fifty, or one hundred dollar bill. The buttons on the right can be used as well for you convenience. Then click cash out and pickupand it'll indicate how much change needs to be given back. IF you have a cash drawer connected to you system, the drawer will pop open.

When you're done giving the customer their change, just click ok on the window and you'll be directed back to the Main Menu.

Chapter- 5

Utilities Menu

At a Glance

In this chapter, we are going to be covering most of the features that come under the **Utilities** menu in Vivaldi Classic. Since some features we already went over, we will be covering just the remaining features from the list.

Item Management

To add items and forced upcharges to your system based on classes you've created or already created for you, you would need to enter into **Item Management**, the first option on the list under the **Utilities menu**.

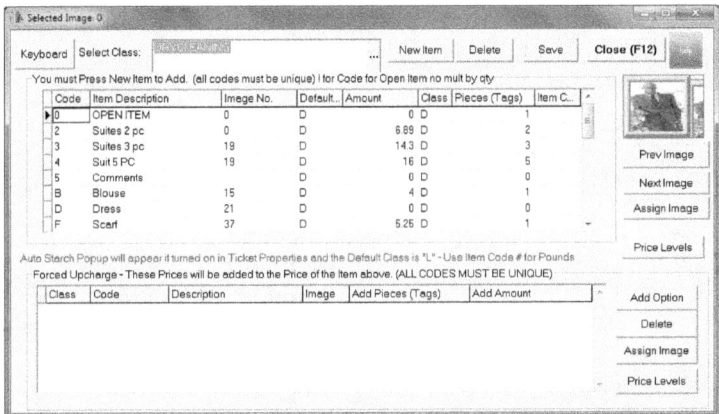

The window is separated into two halves. The upper half is built for all your items. You may scroll through the list if you wish to do so. You can select the class from the **Select Class** field using the (...) button provided. There, a lookup window will appear and you can select the class you wish to modify or add items to.

The bottom half is designed for forced upcharges.

You add new items using the **New Item** button on the top, which will add a new line. There you can include a keyboard code, item description, add an image number using the buttons on the right below the image, the amound of money it costs per item, and the number of pieces per item description.

To assign an image, which will be updated in the writing a ticket window, select the item from the list, then use the **Prev Image** or **Next Image** buttons below the image window on the right and select the image you wish. Once you're done, press the **Assign Image** button below and click **Save**.

Price List/ Multi-level Pricing

If you wish to have different pricelists for different types of clients, such as whole-sale customers, a separate pricelist for a local hotel you're doing business with, or just simply customers that have been coming in with you for several years or are part of the loyalty system, then Vivaldi can do that for you. We will learn later how to add existing customer into one of the price lists.

To access it, you will need to go into **Item Management** under the Utilities **Menu**. There you can select the item(s) from the list that need to be added a price list. Once selected, press the **Price Levels** button on the far right and out will pop a **Price Level** window for the certain item you've selected. Using the buttons provided at the bottom of the window, you may add, modify, or delete price levels from the list.

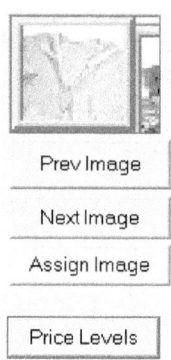

Prev Image

Next Image

Assign Image

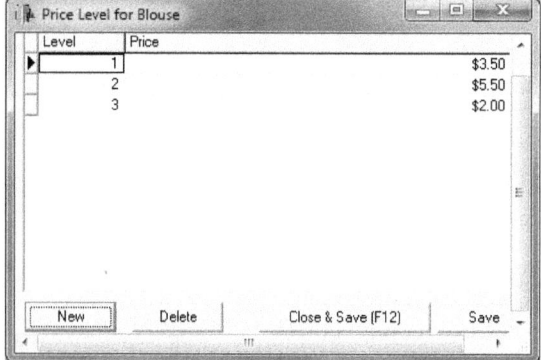

Price Levels

*To apply this to custom-ers, go to that customer's **Customer Information Window**. Under the **Route/Delivery Informa-tion** tab, there's a field called **Price Level**. Select the price level from the list or press 0 for Default.

Global Price Changes

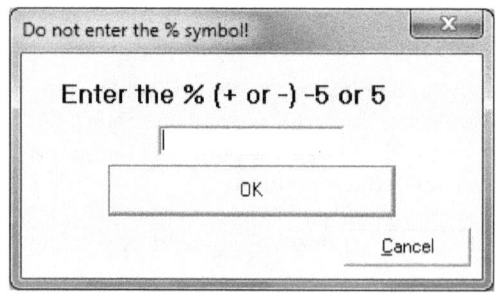

To change the prices of all the pieces at once in a selected class, right mouse click while in the **Item Management** window. Select the **Global Price Change** option. The enter the type of change.

Ex: Enter 10 for a 10 percent change up, or -10 for a 10 percent change down.

Once you're done, press **OK** in the window and save and close the **Item Management** window.

Optional Upcharge Management

If the Optional Upcharge or Color Option is turned on under the **Ticket Properties**, the Optional Upcharge window will appear when you're writing a ticket. You can modify these upcharges by going to the **Utilities** menu and down to **Optional Upcharge Management**.

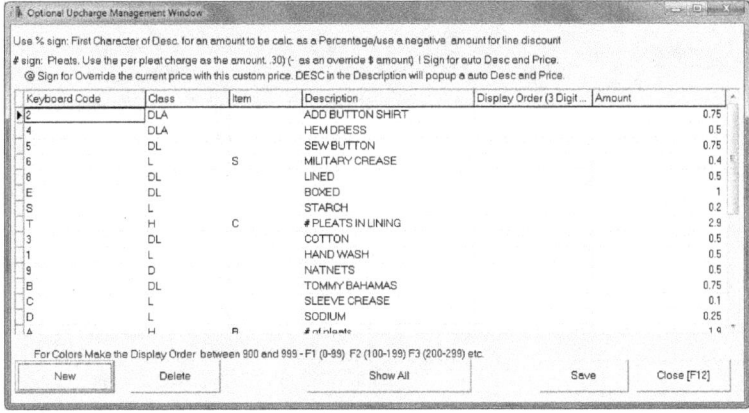

Upcharges must be assigned a unique letter, number, or symbol on the keyboard and linked to a Class or a group of Classes.

If the existing item is assigned to class "D" for Drycleaning and you would like the upcharge to appear whenever a Laundry item is selected, then append the "L" code to the list of Class code.

Ex: DL for Drycleaning and Laundry Items.

*Be sure that the keyboard codes are correct with their assigned **Class Description**. Go to **Class Management** under the **Utilities** menu to check or modify.

Archiving Data

If your computer system that is running Vivaldi Classic seems to be performing slow or for some reason has been slowing down lately. You solution will most likely be attributed to your tickets, which is why Archiving Data is most likely the best guess.

Archiving Data will not only transfer your old data into history, but will ultimately allow your computer to run exponentially faster.

To archive your data, follow these steps:

Step 1: Go to Utilities and then down to Archive Old Tickets (this is how the screen should look like when you get there).

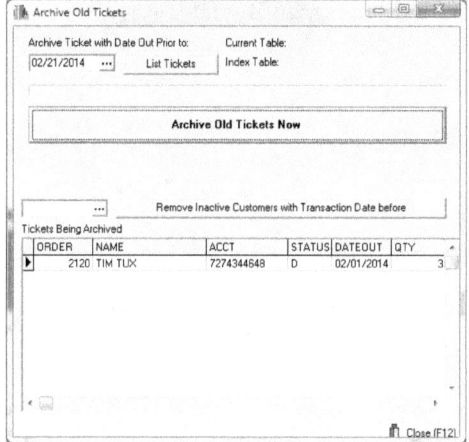

Step 2: You need to set the date. We highly recommend going back 6 months from the current date. This will ensure that all the data prior to that date will be transferred. Yes, we said transferred and not removed into oblivion. Again, they will transfer to the archive history.

Step 3: Once you've added the date using the calendar provided, you can then click on the List Ticket button to the right, which will then automatically list the tickets in the grid that will be archived. Here is where you can then view the tickets & dates and make sure these are the one you want archived.

Step 4: After reviewing, you can then proceed to archive by clicking on the **"archive tickets ready".** This is when you will be provided with plethora of popups asking you important questions. We recommend that you click on the yes or agree positively to the questions, unless there are options that you want to click no. This will not sabotage the entire process. Each process will be done separately.

Remember that when it "removes all the records" it actually transfers all the tickets prior to the cutoff date, and then proceeds to remove them from the ticket file -- no longer giving you access to modify those tickets.

Chapter- 6

Cashdrawer

At a Glance

In this chapter, we will be covering all the essentials in terms of cashdrawer. Once you are finished with this chapter, you will have an understanding at how the cashdrawer works and hopefully work use it to its potential.

Cashdrawer Window

To get to the **Cashdrawer** window, go to the main menu of Vivaldi Classic and select the **Cashdrawer** button.

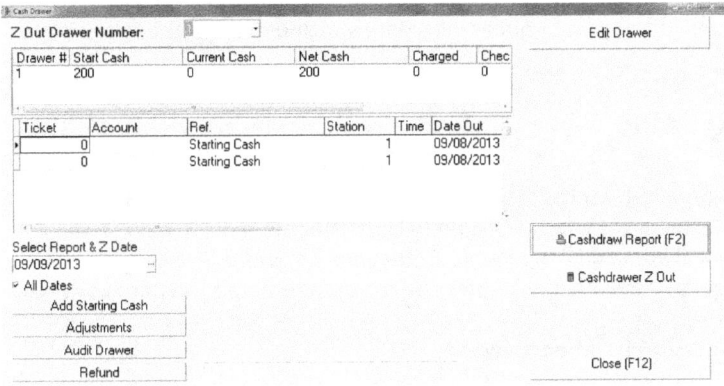

Here you will find all sorts of options you can do with a cashdrawer. You can Z Out the cashdrawer, print a cash reconciliation report, add starting cash, and see most of the money coming in and out of the store using the list above.

Detailed Cashbox Report

To print a detailed Reconciliation Report listing each ticket sorted and group by type of payment, simply Right Mouse Click on on the whitespace of the **Cash Drawer** window and click on **Detail Cashbox Report**.

You will then click on **Preview**, which of course you would then select your **8.5 x 11 in.** printer and print if necessary per day. Then a preview window will appear, where you can print using the first button on the top left.

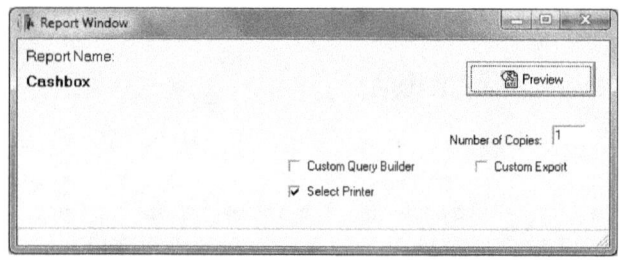

Since we've gone over this at the beginning of this manual, we will simply skim through this section.

To Z Out the cashdrawer, simply press the **Cashdrawer Z Out** button in the **Cashdrawer** window from the main menu. A message will prompt you and ask if you are sure you want to close out this drawer. When you're ready, click **Yes** and the drawer will be closed. You can begin adding your starting cash for the following day.

Add Starting Cash

To add your starting cash for the following day or the day of, click **Add Starting Cash** from the **Cashdrawer** window found in the main menu of Vivaldi Classic. A login window will appear asking you to enter your password. This will most likely be the manager's password. Click **Log In** once you've entered the password.

*As a default, enter 2164 as the password

This will lead you back to the cashdrawer window, where you can now enter the amount on the **Amount** field provided and clicking "Update and Save Amount to Cash Drawer" when you are done.

| Amount | | Update and Save Amount To Cash Drawer |

Chapter- 7

Customer Information Window

At a Glance

In this chapter, we will take a look in detail at the **Customer Information Window** and all it's different tabs, Inventory Control, Outside Processing, Special Orders, Batching Out, Assigning Locations, Assigning Tags at the Counter Tab, and changing an Account Number from a customer.

Customer Information Window

When you click on **Customers** and select a customer from the **Customer Search Window**, you will enter the **Customer Information Window**. As we've mentioned before, the text fields above the tabs is designed for the customer's basic information, but the half below the tabs are designed entirely for the customer's advanced settings. Let's jump into the different types of tabs and what each of the boxes and checkboxes mean.

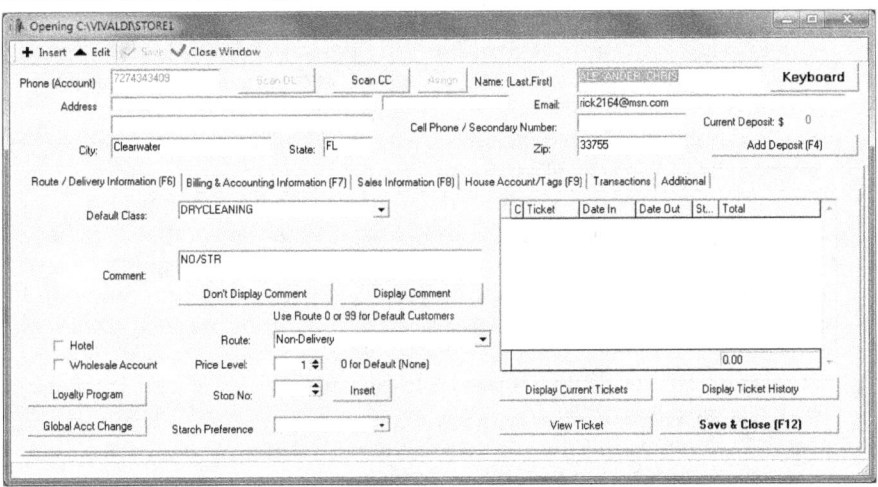

Continued on next page

Route/ Delivery Information

Without further delay, let's describe in a list, what each of the fields and checkboxes mean.

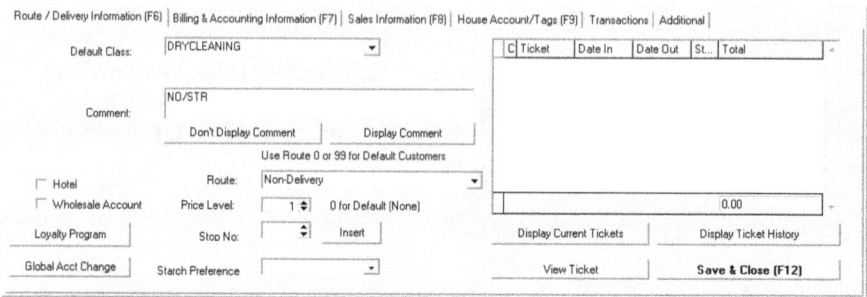

-**Default Class**: This default class allows you to negotiate different pricing for Hotel or Wholesale customers. Whenever a customer with this default class creates a ticket, the default class item list and upcharges will appear.
-**Route:** This is used for the Delivery System (described in a later chapter), which allows you to enter this customer on a given route number for printing and processing **Delivery Manifest**.
-**Price Level:** This will assign this customer to the Item Price Level you created in the Item Management Window. Everytime this customer has a ticket entered, they will receive different prices than others.
-**Stop No.:** This is the Stop on the route, which is used for ordering this customer on the Delivery Manifest.
-**Hotel:** If you have hotels, this is used to tell the system that this is a Hotel Customer. When this box is checked and a ticket is written for this customer, the system will prompt you for the room number and name of guest.
-**Wholesale Account:** This checkbox will allow you to enter a ticket number and name from the agency that is associated with this customer. This will allow the billing for this customer to be the Wholesale Account and will allow all tickets entered under this customer to fall under this wholesale account, which will track their names.
-**Starch Preference:** This preference will appear on the comment area on the screen above when you select this customer.

Billing & Accounting Information

This is where you can add a customer to the accounts receivable system.

Billing Address:		Billing Acct:	7274343409
		% Discount during AR transfer	
Billing City:	Clearwater	Billing State: FL	
Billing Zip:	33755		
Credit Card Number:		Enter Password here then Press Button Below:	
Exp. Date: (MMYY)		Submit Password to Open Discount, Account And Credit Card	

☑ Taxable   ☑ Allow this Customer to be a Charge Account   ... % Discount

☐ Cash Customer Only   This is the Ticket Discount. All Discounts must exist in Coupon Management as Coupons.

Save & Close (F12)

-**Billing Acct:** The billing account needs to be the same as the Account number above. If you enter another account number here, then all orders placed for this customer on the account will be transferred to the new account number.

- **%Discount during AR Transfer**: This will take a percentage off or add a percentage. *Do not enter a % sign. Just the number 10 for a 10% discount will do just fine.

- **%Discount**: This will automatically add a discount to the ticket evertime the customer adds a ticket. This discount will show on the ticket. To enter a discount, you need to enter the Manager's password (Default password is 2164) into the "**Enter Password here then Press Button Below**" then you can click the "**Submit Password to Open Discount, Account And Credit Card.**" This is also where you have access to allow this customer to be a charge account customer using the checkbox provided.

- **Credit Card Number & Exp. Date**: Once you've entered the password, the credit card number and expiration date fields are activated. You can enter their information and Vivaldi Classic will put the card number on file for automatic credit card processing. This is also used for billing the credit card in a batch for Delivery Customer or at the end of the month for credit card customers who wish to be billed monthly from the Accounts receivable (explained in a later chapter).

Sales Information

Birthdate:			Active
YTD Totals:	393.24	Update Yearly with Reset Marketing Dollars	Inactive
No. of Total Items:	80	Total Dollars Spent:	
		First Order Date: 04/22/2009	
Last Transaction:	09/09/2013	Total Loyalty Dollars 54 Reset	

Save & Close (F12)

This tab allows you to view the sales marketing data for this customer. It will keep track of the Loyalty information if they are activated to be in the **Loyalty System** in the **Route/ Delivery Information** tab.

You can add a **Birthdate** so that when they come in and make a transaction on their birthdate, a reminder will pop out and help you celebrate.

YTD: You can see the Year To Date total dollars they've spent with you in this store.

Inventory Control

Let's switch up a little and skip to Inventory Control, which can be accessed using the **Inventory** button on the main menu or **Inventory Control** under the **Office** menu.

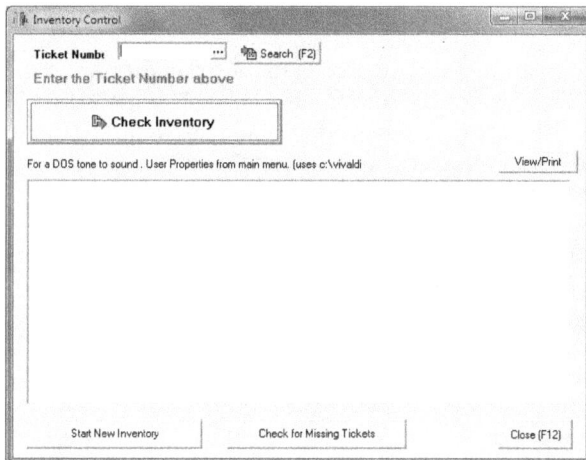

You can use the Inventory Control Module by entering the ticket number by hand (or, as I strongly recommend, use a barcode scanner). You will first need to include the barcode on the tickets. This can be done by modifying the ticket so the ticket number on the top using the barcode font found at www.vivaldi2000.com. For assisstance, Call Vivaldi Classic Technical Support.

After you scan a ticket, the barcode scanner will press the enter key automatically for you and the text "Enter the Ticket Number Above" will change to indicate if the Ticket Number is OK.

If a ticket is found that has been Picked up, Delivered, Voided, or is not currently in the System, this ticket number and the message indicating the problem will appear in the Window. Only those ticket with problems will appear. To Print and Save the list off issues, press the **View/ Print** button on the center right of the window.

After you press the **View/ Print** button, you can select **Save or Print** from the **File** menu in the **Notepad** Window.

Outside Processing

The Outside Processing system can help you indicate that tickets are going to an outside processing center by entering the new location. To get to this window, go to **Outside Processing** under the **Counters** menu.

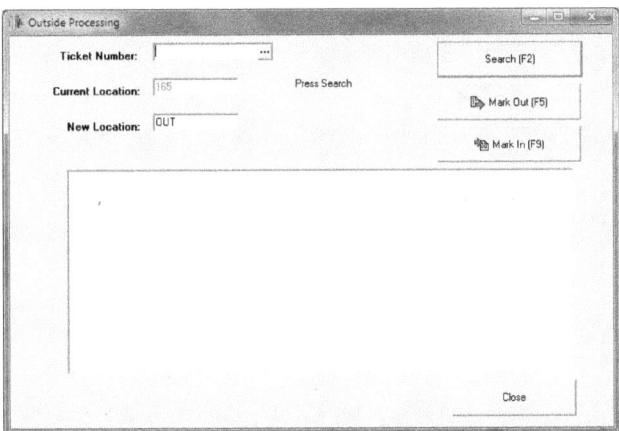

New locations can be codes assigned to each outside processing center or can be in numbers, etc.... Then enter the ticket number or scan the ticket barcode as press the **F5** key or **Mark Out** button. When the item is returned, then press the **F9** key or press the **Mark In** button.

Special Orders

In the Special Orders menu, you can indicate that tickets are special and require special handling or monitoring. You can access this window by going to the **Special Orders** button under the **Counters** menu.

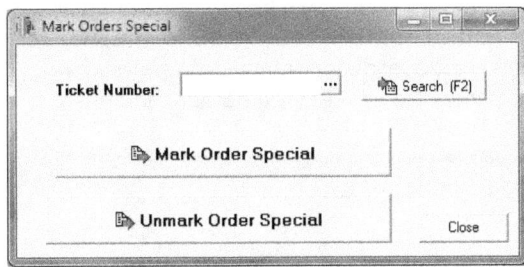

By entering the ticket number using the keyboard or, better yet, barcode scanner, you can **Mark Order Special**. This will allow your report on special orders to the plant.

Assigning Locations

To assign locations to a rack, you can utilize the Assign Location system, which can be accessed using the **Assign Location** from the main menu button. Pressing **F10** is also an option.

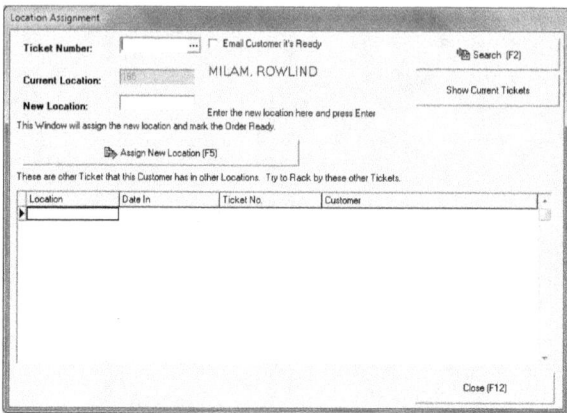

You can begin by inputing or scanning the ticket number onto the provided field above, and then input the location where the ticket will be placed. The **Assign Location** screen will display all other orders and their location in the box below. This is so you can place the order near the other orders.

*If you have a barcode scanner and barcodes on the racks, it may be easier to scan the ticket and then the rack barcode number.

Garment Tag Search

Many cleaners will assign the garment tags at a counter when they are tagging the cloths. To get to this window, go to the **Counter** menu and down to **Garment Tag Search**. Scan the ticket with the barcode reader or enter ticket number by hand. Then you can press enter. Then enter the garment tag number and press enter again.

When you are finished, press the **F12** function key to exit.

Global Account Change

Most cleaners use the phone number for account number. But what happens if you need to change that number? That would create a problem for the system when the customer moves or changes their phone number. The best way to change this instead of creating a new customer and then loosing all the transactions done to their account, is to use the **Global Replace Account Number** system which can be accessed under the **Counter** menu.

This option could also be accessed under the intended customer's information window.

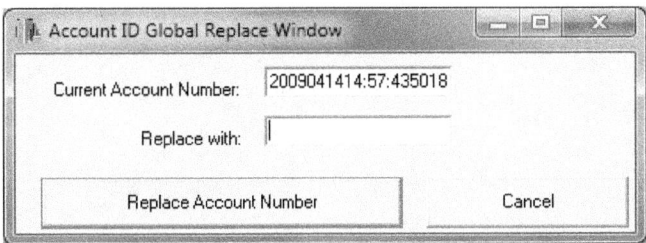

Once the window pops up, you will two fields: a current account number and the number you want to replace it with.

*Remember to place the appropriate hyphens in the phone number.

Mark Tickets Ready

You may be wondering why there's a button called **Mark Tickets Ready** on the main menu. Isn't there a a button called assign a location that does the same thing? The answer is Yes! The mark tickets ready does basically what its sister button does except assign a specific rack location. This is mostly done in case you don't have racks to organize your tickets and items, or are in a rush and just want to mark the ticket out of "in process" and ready to be picked up.

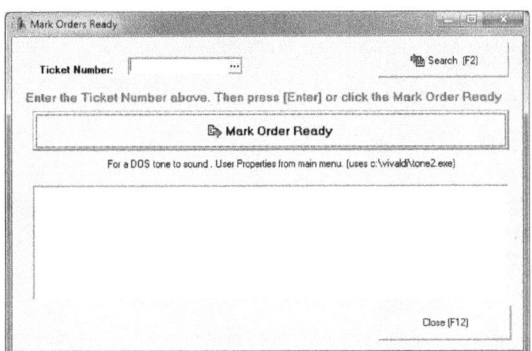

To mark it ready, just go to the window, type or scan in the ticket number, press **Enter** or click the **Mark Order Ready** button down below. Once you're done, click **Close** from the bottom of the window and you're set.

Chapter- 8

Reports

At a Glance

In this chapter will focus entirely on reports in Vivaldi Classic. Believe me when I'll tell you that there are a lot of reports built into the system. First things first, we'll get a feel of where the reports under their respective top menu. Then we will dive into the fun part of this chapter dealing with the Custom Query Builder, which is a module focusing on making your own custom reports.

Custom Query Builder

Vivaldi uses a report writer and within it you can use customer queries prior to printing any reports. Customer query allows you can define specific filters to be used before your print a report. So for instance, let's say you pull up a customer report and want only to see customers from a specific zip code. Custom query allows you to do that.

*Since Custom Query Builder is such an massive module and allow you to virtually pull up any report as long as you input specific parameters or conditions into fields, we will only be able to demostrate one example and then you may challenge yourself into building your own reports for your store.

OK so let's build that report by going to **Reports** up on the menu, going down to **Customer Reports** and clicking on **Customer Listings.** Before we build the report, let's select the **Custom Query Builder** checkbox. This is gonna tell the report writer to pop up the custom query write prior to printing. Let's click the **Preview** button.

A small screen pops up called the Insert Selection Rule window. What you're doing here is telling the report writer that you want to filter the report for a given field for a given or range of value. An easier way to do this is clicking the dot dot dot button the right side of the field. Click the lookup button.

Chapter- 9

Office Menu

At a Glance

As I've mentioned before, the office menu is very complex and has several built-in modules that can be beneficial to managers and users. In this chapter, we will jump into the **Office** menu from the main menu. First, we will focus on the **Accounts Receivable**, a very sophisticated accounts system. Then we will dive into the **Delivery Accounts**, sneak into the **Wholesale Accounts** module, and then learn how to **Merge Multiple Stores** from the **Office** menu. Sit back and get ready for a long chapter.

Accounts Receivable

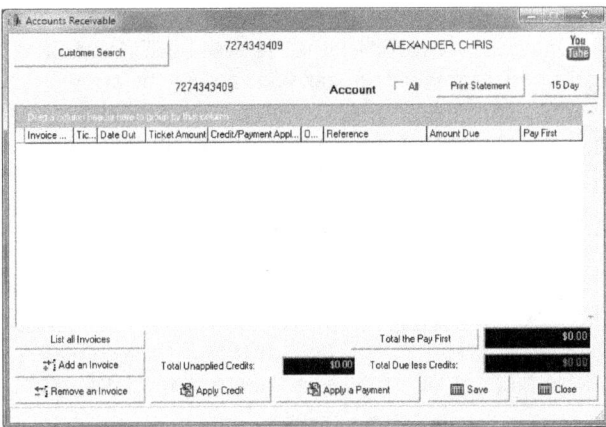

To enter the **Accounts Receivable** window, select it by going to the **Office** menu and then firstly selecting the **Account Receivable Maintenance**. You will be asked to select a customer from the following list. You can search by Customer Name, Account ID, or Phone number. Once you've found your customer, double click on the customer and the customer transactions will appear called the **Accounts Receivable** window.

To apply a payment, press the **Apply a Payment** button down at the bottom of the screen.

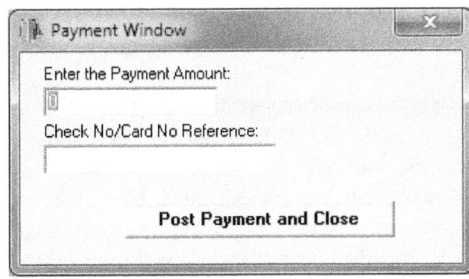

The payment window will appear. Enter the dollar amount and the check or card number for reference using the fields provided. The reference number will appear on the statement. You may also make comments such as credit to account or reference to a coupon or comp. Once you're done click **Post Payment and Close**.

After the close button is pressed, the system will ask if you would like this credit applied to **Open Invoices**.

-If you select Yes, the system will apply the amount paid to the oldest ticket first and apply as much as possible to each ticket until the credit is used.
-If you select No, the system will keep this payment on AR as a standing credit and will reflect as much on the invoice adjusting and current or future debt.

All account customers must have a billing account for the account system to work. So go to the customer's information window and go apply their billing and credit card information.

Printing Statements for Customers

To print statments, select the **Accounts Receivable - > AR Statements** from the Office menu. A small window will pop out. Just click the **Preview** button and all the statements for each Account Customer will appear. you can use the arrow keys to select a specific customer, then press the page button to print only that page

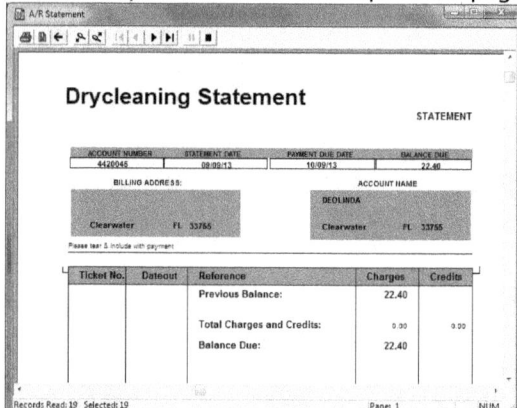

or press the printer button to print all the documents.

You can also select the **Aged AR Report** from the menu and simply press the preview button with any date in the fields. This will list all the account customers and total the aged values.

Wholesale Accounts

To setup a wholesale account, you must first enter the **Billing Information** tab under the customer's **Information Window**. There you have the option of turning on the **Wholesale Account** checkbox.

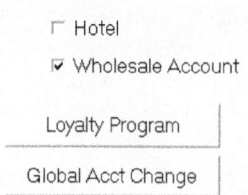

You may then use the window called **Wholesale Accounts** window under the **Office** menu to enter the rest of the customer's information such as discounts or parent relationships to other customers. Each ticket written will receive the discount % found on the Billing Information tab. The wholesale discount will be used in the wholesale statement taking a total % off the total of all orders.

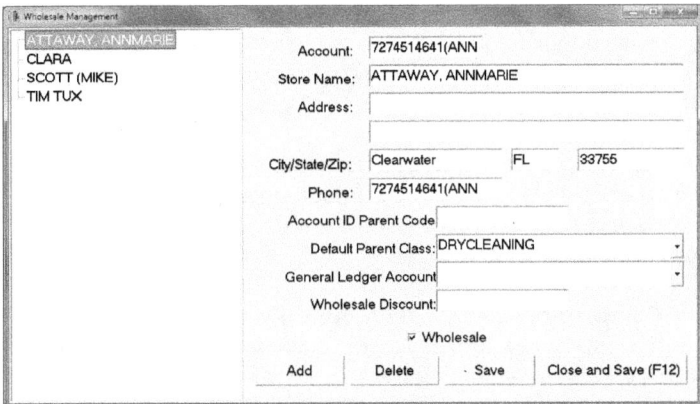

It is best to set up a new class and price list for each wholesale, since most wholesale prices are negotiated individually and then set the default class on the customer to that class.

Delivery Management

The Delivery module focuses on those customers who drop off their items and want them delivered at a convenient location and/or the store has a a truck follow a designated route to pickup and deliver tickets. The following process will work with all delivery customers. Since the Delivery module of Vivaldi Classic could be complex for most customers, we will spread it out into several steps. Let's begin!

Step 1: Setting up Routes

First things first, you must decide on your route schedule and number of routes

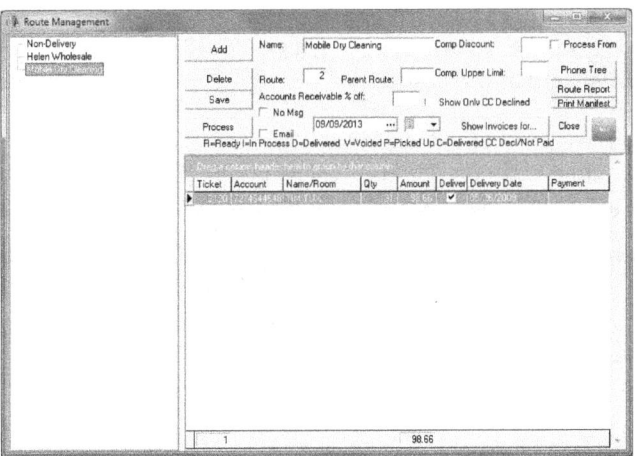

based on the truck route and the day or time of delivery. To get to this screen, you must go to **Office -> Delivery Management -> Manage Delivery Manifests.** Remember that routes must not use the number 0 or 99. All other numbers are available.

Route 0 is reserved General Non-Delivery Customers. The default route for counter systems should alwats be 0. That way all the counter non-delivery customers will not be placed on a delivery manifest. This will prevent Vivaldi Classic from asking if you would like the ticket delivered every time a counter customer is selected during the add ticket process.

To add a route press the **Add** button. Remember to assign a route number that is not currently being used. Only one route per number. Once you're done, click Save. You can indicate the parent route by placing the parent route number in the **Parent Route Field**.

The **Comp Discount, Comp. Upper Limit, and Accounts Receivable %** off are used primarily for hotels. You would normally assign each hotel a separate route number and all rtickets written for employees, managers, or hotel guests would be given a separate customer under that route all linked to the same route.

Step 2: Adding Customer to Your Routes

Now that you have your routes assigned. You now need to assign customers to those certain routes. You can do this by going to a specific customer's information

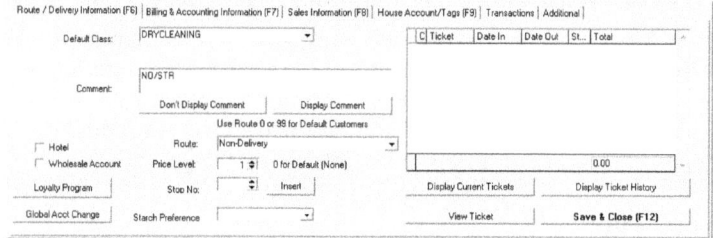

window under the **Route/ Delivery Information** tab. Or you can reassign current customers to the newly created routes.

If this customer is a hotel customer, you will need to place a check in the hotel checkbox on the **Route/ Delivery Information** tab.

> *If the customer charges will be charged to a credit card, you will want to enter the standing credit carn number in the credit card field under **Billing Information** tab as well as the **Expiration date** using the appropriate format.
> * If the customer will be recieving a statement from you for their charges, you will need to indicate that this is an Account customer, which can be found under the Billing Information tab. Vivaldi Classic will transffer the charge after the delivery manifest has been processed and the ticket has been delivered and the cash drawer has been z'd out for the out.

Step 3:

In this step, you may begin writing tickets for the customer you've just assigned to a route number, which we covered in the previous step.

Now, the ticket is written for this customer. The system will ask the user if this ticket is to be delivered. Remember that even though the customer is a delivery customer Vivaldi does confirm that this ticket is going to be delivered. The clothes are then processed.

Step 4: Marking Tickets Ready

The Ticket is marked ready. This process is critical for delivery. You can default the tickets to Ready when the ticket is added then the delivery system will simply use the dateout as the indicator that the ticket is to be included on the manifest but this becomes difficult to manage. By using the Mark order ready you can always be assured that only those tickets ready for delivery will be included in the manifest.

Step 5: Process a Ticket

Now let's process the ticket for the customer you've selected and that you've just written tickets for.

While writing the ticket the following box will appear, answer Yes.

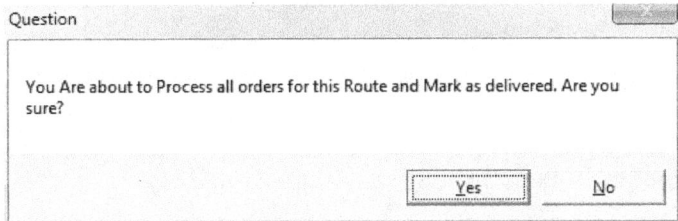

The following ticket or tickets will be processed and will be added unto their respective accounts where they will be charged through credit card automatically through X-Charge.

Step 6: Printing the Delivery Manifest

The following step would be to print the **Delivery Manifest** each day for the routes for that day.

*Note that the Delivery Date is set for the Date Out schedule of the ticket we entered. This will list all tickets associated with customers on routes that are scheduled for delivery on that day. This delivery manifest will list all tickets even those that are not ready. This will allow the driver to check on status of tickets that are not ready and perhaps expedite

Step 7: Processing

You will receive a separate page for each route.

The driver takes the Manifest and Signs the bottom after verifying that all the tickets are loaded on the truck.

After each item is delivery he/she will indicate the status after each item. D indicates delivered. Blank indicates that he/she could not delivery the ticket and that ticket is returning to the plant for the next scheduled delivery date.

One the Manifest is returned to the plant the driver or accounting person enters the **Office – Delivery management – Process Delivery Manifest** option on the top menu.

Select the Route on the tree on the left and confirm that the Date is the date you want to process.

By using the right mouse button a popup menu will appear that will allow you to reschedule any ticket that you have currently selected 1,2,3,4,5 or a week later than the current system date. After you select one of the options the ticket will be removed from the list and will not appear again until you select the new date in the date box next to the Process button.

Once the list only lists those tickets that have been delivered then press the Process button. You can select I status (In Process) tickets by selecting I from the drop down or change the date to process tickets prior or in the future. This is useful if the driver returned too late or if you wish to Process the following day.

After Pressing Process the following button will appear to confirm that you want to process this route.

After the Process is complete for this route the following message will appear:

You will note in Back Office – Cash Drawer that the Totals for the tickets in A/R and Credit Cards have included the Tickets for this Route. Also the Edit Ticket Status of this ticket indicates Delivered.

Batching Out

To get to the Batching Out menu, select **Batch Out** button under the **Office** menu.

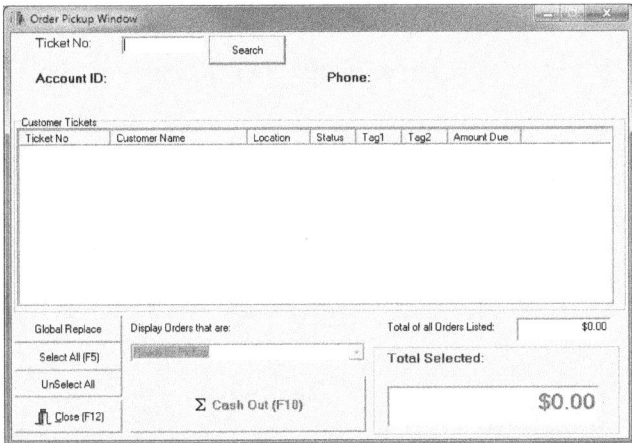

Vivaldi will allow you to batch out many tickets using the barcode reader or entering by hand. This works great for wholesale tickets or when you prefer not to use the cashdrawer/ pickup modules. Basically, you enter the ticket numbers regardless of the customer then cash out all at once. Make sure the tickets are entered in groups and cashed out in groups according to payment type. To batch out select the Pickup by **Ticket No. (F9)** from the left menu or press the F9 function key. Then scan each ticket, then cash out.

Merging Multiple Stores

You can create a Consolidated store across the internet on a server by installing Vivaldi on a server with a dedicated IP Address, sharing the C drive and creating a store 99 on that server. Then on the Client system enter the System Properties and the "Pickup/Store" tab and enter the Virtual Pathname into the "Path to Consoliation Data" field. See the example below.

When you wish to consolidate the data from this store and merge it with other stores simple select the Menu Office then Select the "Update Main Office" option.

Prepayment Discount

To set an automatic percentage for prepayment, enter the **Ticket Properties** and set the **Auto Discount for Prepayment** % for the percentage you wish to give prepayment tickets. You also need to set the percentage in the **Coupon Manage-**

ment window under the **Utilities** menu as a percetage coupon. This is required for tracking of all percentages.

Coupon Management

To to to the couon management window, go to **Coupon Management** from the **Utilities** menu.

This will prompt you to this window. You will see a couple columns lined up: the coupon desciption colun, the dollar amount column, a percentage amount column, a maximum amount column, and the applicable classes.

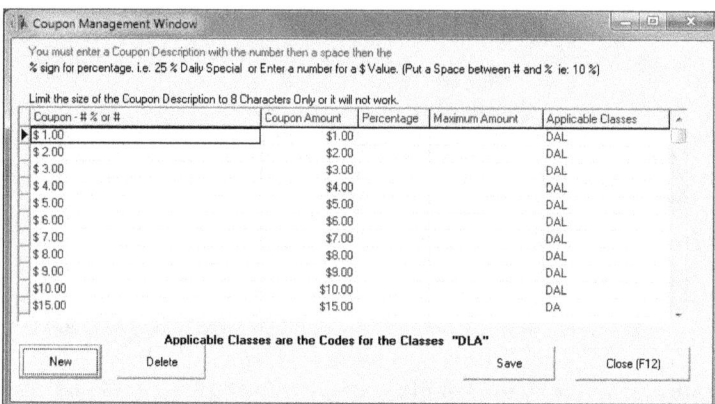

Let's break it up and begin describing what each of the columns do and what you can input in them. Then later you may add your own information in them or create new classes.

1. **Coupon - $ or %**: this first column is where you basically add your description so that when you do apply a discount to a customer, you will know what will be applied. Remember that this is just a description column, meaning that what ever you type in here, won't give a command to the system, that what the second and third column do.

2. **Coupon Amount**: This column is where you tell Vivaldi Classic what dollar amount you would like to give as a coupon. Go ahead and type in a dollar amount including the "$" sign and you're set.

3. **Percentage:** This column is basically like its sister column to the left, but instead of dollar amount, just type in the percetange amount without having to add it's appropriate symbol.

4. **Maximum Amount**: This column is specially designed for the percentage discount, since some managers don't like to exceed a certain amount of discount, you can add it here. Ex: a 10% discount should not exceed a $5 subtractive from the total amount.

5. **Applicable Classes**: This is by far the most impotant column besides adding your discount. Here you assign the classes you want your discounts or coupons to apply. Using the defaulted keyboard codes (or codes you made yourself), Vivaldi Classic will know which discounts are set for which classes.

Chapter-10

Loyalty System

At a Glance

In this chapter, we will be focusing on the loyalty program built in the Vivaldi Classic system. The Loyalty System is quite sophisticated and can keep track of customer total sales and can print automatic coupons when a customer has reached a level you have assigned. It also keeps track of total number of tickets and prints automatic coupons using the ticket printer. As a treat for the customer, the Loyalty System can credit the customer with a dollar credit that can be redeemed automatically on their next pickup. Alright, let's get to it!!

Loyalty Information on System Properties

Before we can use the loyalty system, we need to turn it on and configure it by going to the **Advanced** tab of the **System Properties.**

Loyalty Information

Loyalty Level (by $ or quantity amount) `100`

Enter ALL for Item and Class if all Items will count

for Item Code `ALL`   and Class code `ALL`

☐ All New Customers

☐ Enterprise

☐ Mark Tickets except for Today

☐ Loyalty Points by Order Quantity

☑ or Loyalty by $ Total

Loyalty Reward $ (0 for Coupon only)

`10`

There are three steps:

Step 1: Loyalty Level

Using the text field provided called the **Loyalty Level (by $ or quantity amount**). Here you can enter the amount the customer will need to meet before they can be rewarded with loyalty dollars.

Step 2: Loyalty by Order or $

If you are going to be measuring the loyalty point by either quantity or dollar amount, then you must indicate using the check marks provided. You cannot check on both boxes at once because it will confuse the system, so please be careful.

You can also enter the class code and item code using their respective fields. If you don't remember what the class codes are, visit the **Class Management** window to check the keyboard codes.

Step 3: Loyalty Reward $

You can reward customer with loyalty points by giving them either dollar amounts or coupons. Using the number field provided called **"Loyalty Reward $ (0 for Coupon only)**, you can enter the amount.

Ex: For every $100 they spent with you, then will receive 10 dollars in reward dollars.

Assign Customers to the Loyalty Program

Basically, everything we just mentioned would not work if we don't assign customers to the loyalty program. Just go to the customer's information window that can be accessed using the **Customers** window in the main menu. Under the **Route/Delivery Information** tab, there is a button on the lower left called **Loyalty Program.**

To add the customer to the loyalty program, simply click the button and they are automatically assigned to the system.

If you choose to turn on the loyalty reward dollars, the dollars will be placed in the **House Account** tab of the **Customer** window in the Due field as a negative dollar amount. You can change this or remove the amount any time you wish.

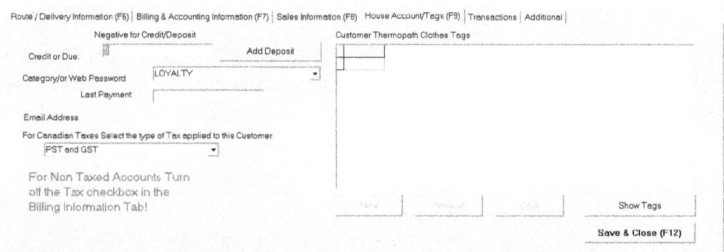

Loyalty Report Customization

If you need to customize your loyalty report, technical support may do that for you as long as you have a 32 bit PC.

Chapter-11
Hardware and Software
At a Glance

In this chapter we'll get into the hardware and software outside of Vivaldi Classic and see what you need to do to get your system up and running. First we'll take a look at the printers and then the little things from Adjusting Memory to Archiving Data.

Setting Database Configurations Settings

There are two attributes that need to be configured under Borland Database Engine on each client. To set the database attributes, enter BDE Administrator found under the Administrator folder in the Window Control Panel. Once in the BDE Administrator, select the configuration tab. There select the INIT node on the tree on the left.

The two settings that need to be configured are the SHARED, that needs to be set to TRUE. The FILES HANDLE needs to be configured to 50 handles for each client on the network. (Ex: If there are 3 stations on the current network, set the files handled to 150.)

Clear Out Data

!!!WARNING: THIS WILL REMOVE ALL CUSTOMERS, TICKETS, ACCOUNTS RECEIVABLE, AND TICKET HISTORY FROM VIVALDI CLASSIC.

*This should only be done when newly purchasing the system and want to clear out existing demo data. Clear our Data does not remove classes, items and upcharges. It should be turned off in access control once you've actively started using the system.

To clear it, you can access the window under the **Utilities** menu and down to its respective button. Once you're on the window, press the button. You will be prompted with a warning message if you want to fully remove data. Click Ok and you're done.

Network Setup

The network setup is primarily used for setting up multiple stations in a single

location. Networking Vivaldi Classic is primariloy used in a client-server situation, where the server can be any non-dedicated station on the network, but configured to share the database.
Vivaldi doesnt require a dedicated server, but one of the stations must share the local "C" drive, in order for the clients to map that drive to access the data with read/write permissions.

Here are the steps required to map out a drive on Windows 7:

Step 1: Wired Connection

The first step to setting up a network is to make sure that all computers are configured on a local LAN, using non-wireless connections, meaning that each computer needs to be connected through a cable to a hub or a common router.

(Wireless connections are not stable and tend to corrupt data. **PLEASE AVOID**)

Step 2:

All the computers on the network need to be configured to use the same Windows workgroup.

(Please avoid using Windows domains, unless you are a skilled certified network administrator)

Users from each client need to have complete read/write access to the local "C " drive and subfolders on the folder. Please make sure you've shared the local server "C" drive and granted permission to the entire drive to all users on the network.

Step 3:

Setup each client computer by mapping the server's local "C" drive to a local drive letter. (Vivaldi Classic usually uses "V" or "Z")

Please make sure when you create the mapping, that you save the username and password and indicate that this mapping should reconnect automatically at login.

Step 4:

Install the Vivaldi "setup.exe" and the most current upgrade on each of the computers on the network, including the server. Clear out the demo data on each computer and optimize and cleanup on each station.

Step 5:

Enter the **System Properties** under the **Help** menu under each of the clients, changing the drive letter under the **Store Data Path** and Store Pat from the local "C" drive to map drive letter, retaining the current directory paths.

Step 6:
To complete the setup on a client, exit Vivaldi Classic and open it back up to test that the mapping and the permissions have been setup properly. Attemt to add a customer from each client computer to test the read/write access.

(Any errors opening the application indicates that the mapping or permission was not created properly.)

Ticket and Tag Printer Configuration

Ticket/ Receipt Printer

Vivaldi Classic uses three types of printers. Noticably, the first type is the receipt/ ticket printer. This printer is typically a thermal printer with an automatic printer cutter. We currently recommend the **Star TSP100 USB** . USB is highly recommended for all computer since all new computers ship with USB ports. The **STAR TSP100** uses stardard **3 inch** thermal paper that can be purchased at any office supply store.

Tag Printer

Vivaldi has the option of using a tag printer that prints along side the ticket when the ticket is created. The tag printer is not required when using Vivaldi if you choose to use the standard preprinted tags. The tag printer recommended by Vivaldi is the **Star TSP700 USB.** This printer includes an autocutter that can be configured to cut the tags to a quarter inch to a full inch in height. This printer should be set as the default printer on any client where the printer is connected in order to properly download the printer configuration.

The paper required to print tags can be found at *cleanersupply.com*. Purchase the computer 3 inch computer tag rolls and then choose your paper color option.

Report Printer

Vivaldi reports are configured to print on an **8.5 x 11 inch** printer, and therefore required an appropriate paper sized printer. Any printer supported by Windows is compatible with the Vivaldi report.

Setting Up Automatic Cashdrawer

Most automatic cashdrawer have a telephone-like cable that connects to the back of a POS printer.

(If your automatic cashdrawer has a serial connection, you will need to call Vivaldi Support to help install.)

Once the cashdrawers are connected, you will need to share the printer that the cashdrawer is connected to. Vivaldi typically uses the **STAR TSP100** as the referent cashdrawer connection.

To share the printers, open the **Printers and Devices** in the Windows **Control Panel.** Under the sharing tab, select the Select this Printer checkbox. Name the printer share name as "ticket."

The cashdrawer is opened using a batch file named "cashdrawer.bat" located in the "C:\Vivaldi" folder. You will need to modify this file if the cashdrawer is located on a different computer or you've named the share name differently. Lastly, to turn on the cashdrawer, enter the **System Properties** from the **Help** menu and select the checkbox: "Use Automatic Cashdrawer."

Integrated Credit Card Processing/ X-Charge

Vivaldi Classic includes an integrated credic card processing software, connecting to the X-charge credit card processing network. X-Charge links to you bank's merchant account immediately depositing your credit card charges to your bank.

To setup the X-Charge credit card processing system, you will need to call an X-Charge sale representative and apply for an account.

X-Charge can be reached at (800) 637-8268 ext.111

Vivaldi's integrated credit card processing, once set up, will prompt you to swipe the customer's credit card any time you pay or prepay a ticket from Vivaldi Classic. Integrated credit card processing is also linked to the Vivaldi delivery system automatically posting charges of delivery orders to the associated customer's credit on file (found under Billing and Information tab) when the order is delivered.

Credit card processing is also integrated into the accounts receivable modules allowing you to autmatically charge total monthly balances to a customer's credit card on file.

Remote Login/ Teamviewer

Teamviewer is a remote desktop software that is user friendly and comes with little costs. This software will allow the Vivaldi Team to provide support by logging in to your system remotely. You may create an account after you install the program. Below we provide step-by-step instructions on how to install the software on your system:

How to Install TeamViewer

To install the software you must first visit the website by going to www.teamviewer.com and by downloading the software by clicking on the **green button** on the page or by clicking this download link. Once you open the file, you may be asked to give access in order to install the software. Just click **Run**.

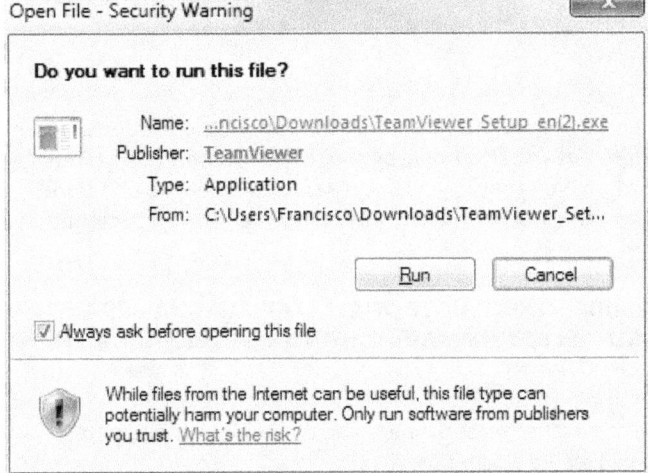

After you run the file, you will be presented with this screen. Based on the radio buttons selected, make sure you select **Install** under the "How do you want to proceed" option and **Personal / Non-commercial** use for the "How do you want to use TeamViewer" option below. Just click **Accept - finish** once you're done with this screen.

(go to next page to see image)

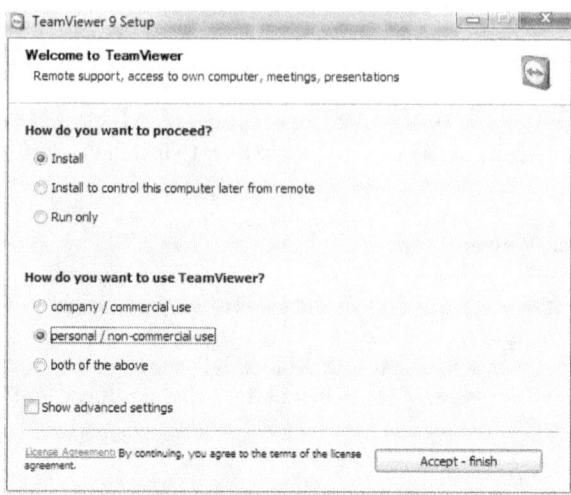

Next, you see a new screen where different parts of the windows are labeled. After that, there will be two different windows side-by-side: One that contains your ID and Password and one where you may login to you account. If you haven't done so, create an account using the link provided at the bottom of the right screen, which looks like this:

IMPORTANT NOTE: BE SURE TO KEEP NOTE OF ALL YOUR USERNAMES AND PASSWORDS EITHER INITIALLY STORED AND THAT YOU'VE CREATED, AS IT WILL BE NECESSARY FOR SUPPORT.

You will be presented with another screen where you may fill out all the details. On the next screen you will include your password.

After this, you should be setup and ready to use. If you are having trouble installing TeamViewer, please don't hesitate to call Vivaldi Customer Support at +1(760) 282-4421.

www.ingramcontent.com/pod-product-compliance
Lightning Source LLC
Chambersburg PA
CBHW070227210526

45169CB00023B/1013